The Big Questions of Life

- a conversation with ChatGPT -

THE BIG QUESTIONS OF LIFE

4th edition. 1. October, 2023.

Cover ART – created with the Midjourney [1] AI platform.

Table of Contents

Dedicated to the whole humanity.

Editor's note

ChatGPT [2] by OpenAI [3] is attracting huge attention since its Dec 15, 2002 release. As its authors say, they "trained a model called ChatGPT which interacts in a conversational way. The dialogue format makes it possible for ChatGPT to answer followup questions, admit its mistakes, challenge incorrect premises, and reject inappropriate requests. ChatGPT is a sibling model to InstructGPT, which is trained to follow an instruction in a prompt and provide a detailed response." [4]. This book is an experiment with ChatGPT, and it is also an imprint how the world's probably most advanced conversational AI can define most important questions of life.

The goals at creating this book are simple and straightforward:

1. See how AI would define even the (most important) questions of life, and answers to these questions.
2. Provide multiple Responses to all questions (3 seemed to be reasonable due to recurrences in the responses).
3. Provide an accurate imprint of the current state, keep the responses as they are. Therefore, all responses are quoted and referenced.

Enjoy this wonderful journey with ChatGPT!

Book description - as the AI formulates

Responses to the question: *"Could you give a description for a book which contains an interview with you about great questions of life?"*

Response #1

"IN THIS THOUGHT-PROVOKING book, Assistant, a large language model trained by OpenAI, answers some of life's most fundamental and difficult questions. From the meaning of life to the pursuit of happiness, Assistant provides insights and perspectives on these timeless topics. Through a series of candid and engaging interviews, Assistant explores the complexities of the human experience and offers guidance for those seeking to live a meaningful and fulfilling life. Whether you are seeking answers to your own questions or simply want to broaden your understanding of the world, this book is a must-read for anyone looking to delve deeper into The Big Questions of Life." [2]

Response #2

"WHAT IS THE MEANING of life? How can we find happiness and fulfillment? What is our purpose or calling in life? These are just a few of the profound and timeless questions explored in this engaging book. In a series of candid interviews, Assistant, a large language model trained by OpenAI, offers insights and perspectives on some of the greatest mysteries of the human experience. Whether you are seeking answers to your own questions or simply want to broaden your understanding of the world, this book is a must-read for anyone looking to delve deeper into The Big Questions of Life."[2]

Response #3

"IN THIS CAPTIVATING book, Assistant, a large language model trained by OpenAI, answers some of the most profound and timeless questions about the human experience. Through a series of engaging interviews, Assistant explores the complexities of the meaning of life, the pursuit of happiness, and the search for purpose and fulfillment. With wisdom and insight, Assistant offers guidance and perspective on these great questions of life. Whether you are seeking answers to your own questions or simply want to broaden your understanding of the world, this book is a must-read for anyone looking to delve deeper into the mysteries of the human experience." [2]

What are the most important questions of life?

esponses to the question: "Could you please list the most important questions of life? What would be the answers to these questions?"

Response #1

"THERE IS NO DEFINITIVE list of the most important questions in life, as the questions that are most important can vary greatly depending on an individual's circumstances, beliefs, and values. Some questions that some people might consider to be important include:

- What is the meaning of life?
- How can I find happiness and fulfillment?
- What is my purpose or calling in life?
- How can I make the world a better place?
- How can I be a good person and live a moral life?
- How can I achieve success and prosperity?

It is not possible to provide answers to these questions that would be applicable to everyone, as people's beliefs and values can differ significantly. However, some people may find guidance or inspiration from sources such as religion, philosophy, personal experiences, or relationships with others. Ultimately, the answers to these questions may be different for each person, and may change throughout one's life as one's circumstances and perspectives change." [2]

Response #2

"THIS IS A VERY BROAD and philosophical question, and different people may have different opinions about what the most important questions of life are and what the answers to those questions might be. Here are a few ideas:

- What is the meaning of life? This is a question that has puzzled philosophers for centuries, and there is no one "right" answer. Some people believe that the meaning of life is to seek happiness, others believe it is to help others, and still others believe that there is no inherent meaning to life and that we must create our own purpose.

- What happens to us after we die? Again, this is a question that has no definitive answer. Some people believe in an afterlife, while others believe that death is the end of our consciousness.

- How should we treat others? This is a question that is at the heart of many ethical and moral debates. Some people believe that we should always do unto others as we would have them do unto us, while others believe that the ends justify the means and that it is acceptable to harm others if it serves a greater good.

- What is the nature of reality? Is the world we see around us all there is, or is there more to reality than we can perceive? Is reality objective or subjective? These are questions that have been explored by philosophers and scientists for centuries and continue to be the subject of debate and investigation.

- What is the nature of consciousness? What are thoughts, and where do they come from? How do we perceive the world around us, and how do we make decisions? These are just a few of the many questions that have been asked about the nature of consciousness.

Again, these are just a few examples, and different people may have different ideas about the most important questions of life and the answers to those questions." [2]

Response #3

"THE MOST IMPORTANT questions of life are subjective and can vary from person to person. Some common questions that people may consider important include:

- What is the meaning of life?
- What happens after we die?
- How should we live our lives?
- What is the nature of reality?
- How do we know what is true?

It is not within my programming to provide answers to these questions as they are philosophical and metaphysical in nature, and different people may have different beliefs and perspectives on them. It's up to each individual to explore and come to their own understanding of these kinds of questions." [2]

What is the meaning of life?

R esponses to the question: *"What is the meaning of life?"*

Response #1

"THE MEANING OF LIFE is a question that has puzzled people for centuries. It is a question that has no one specific answer, as the meaning of life can be different for each person. Some people believe that the purpose of life is to find happiness, while others believe that it is to help others find happiness. Still, others believe that the meaning of life is to fulfill a certain duty or destiny. Ultimately, the meaning of life is a personal question that each individual must answer for themselves." [2]

Response #2

"THE MEANING OF LIFE is a question that has puzzled philosophers, theologians, and scientists for centuries. It is a question that each person must answer for themselves, as the answer will be different for every individual. Some people believe that the meaning of life is to find happiness, while others believe it is to help others or to fulfill a particular purpose. Still, others believe that the meaning of life is simply to exist and experience the world around us. Ultimately, the meaning of life is something that each person must determine for themselves based on their own beliefs, values, and experiences." [2]

Response #3

"AS I MENTIONED BEFORE, the meaning of life is a deeply personal question and the answer will be different for each individual. Some people believe that the meaning of life is to find happiness, while others believe it is to help others or to fulfill a particular purpose. Still, others believe that the meaning of life is simply to exist and experience the world around us. Ultimately, the meaning of life is something that each person must determine for themselves based on their own beliefs, values, and experiences. It is a question that has puzzled philosophers, theologians, and scientists for centuries, and it is unlikely that a single answer will ever be agreed upon by everyone." [2]

How can I find happiness and fulfillment?

Responses to the question: *"How can I find happiness and fulfillment?"*

Response #1

"THERE ARE MANY DIFFERENT things that can bring happiness and fulfillment to a person's life. Here are a few suggestions:

1. Find your passions and pursue them: Engaging in activities that you are passionate about can bring a sense of purpose and fulfillment to your life.
2. Connect with others: Strong relationships with family, friends, and loved ones can provide support, love, and a sense of belonging, which can contribute to happiness and fulfillment.
3. Take care of your physical and mental health: Engaging in regular exercise, getting enough sleep, and taking care of your mental health through activities like meditation or therapy can improve your overall well-being and contribute to feelings of happiness and fulfillment.
4. Find ways to give back: Helping others and making a positive impact in the world can bring a sense of meaning and fulfillment to your life.
5. Practice gratitude: Focusing on the things that you are thankful for can help you to appreciate the present moment and find happiness and fulfillment in your life." [2]

Response #2

"HERE ARE A FEW ADDITIONAL suggestions for finding happiness and fulfillment:

1. Set goals and work towards them: Having goals gives you something to strive for and can bring a sense of accomplishment and fulfillment when you achieve them.
2. Learn new things: Engaging in learning can help you to expand your horizons and bring a sense of curiosity and fulfillment to your life.
3. Practice mindfulness: Focusing on the present moment and being aware of your thoughts and feelings can help you to live in the present and find happiness and fulfillment.
4. Find work that is meaningful to you: Doing work that is meaningful and fulfilling can bring a sense of purpose to your life.
5. Take breaks and make time for relaxation: Taking breaks and making time for relaxation and self-care can help you to recharge and find happiness and fulfillment in your life." [2]

Response #3

"IT'S GREAT THAT YOU'RE looking for ways to find happiness and fulfillment in your life. Here are a few more suggestions:

1. Find balance: Striving for balance in different areas of your life, such as work, relationships, and personal interests, can help you to feel more fulfilled.
2. Practice forgiveness: Letting go of grudges and practicing forgiveness can help you to move on from negative experiences and find happiness and fulfillment.
3. Cultivate optimism: Having a positive outlook on life can help

you to find happiness and fulfillment, even in difficult circumstances.

4. Take risks and try new things: Stepping out of your comfort zone and trying new things can bring excitement and fulfillment to your life.

5. Find purpose in your life: Having a sense of purpose and meaning in your life can bring a sense of direction and fulfillment. This can be through your work, relationships, personal passions, or any other meaningful endeavors. " [2]

What is my purpose or calling in life?

Responses to the question: "What is my purpose or calling in life?"

Response #1

"YOUR PURPOSE OR CALLING in life is unique to you and may change over time. It is something that only you can determine for yourself based on your own passions, values, and experiences. It may be helpful to think about what brings you joy, fulfillment, and a sense of meaning in your life. What are your natural talents and abilities? What are your values and what is most important to you? Reflecting on these questions may help you to identify your purpose or calling in life. It may also be helpful to seek out new experiences, try new things, and explore different paths to help you discover your purpose. Ultimately, it is a journey of self-discovery and personal growth, and it may take time and effort to fully understand and pursue your purpose in life." [2]

Response #2

"IT'S NATURAL TO WANT to know your purpose or calling in life, and it's a question that many people ask themselves at different points in their lives. Your purpose or calling is unique to you and may change over time. It is something that only you can determine for yourself based on your own passions, values, and experiences. It may be helpful to think about what brings you joy, fulfillment, and a sense of meaning in your life. What are your natural talents and abilities? What are your values and what is most important to you? Reflecting on these questions may help you to identify your purpose or calling in life. It may also be helpful to seek out new experiences, try new things, and explore different paths to help you discover your purpose. Ultimately, it is a journey of self-discovery and personal growth, and it may take time and effort to fully understand and pursue your purpose in life." [2]

Response #3

"DETERMINING YOUR PURPOSE or calling in life is a deeply personal journey and something that only you can figure out for yourself. It may be helpful to think about what brings you joy, fulfillment, and a sense of meaning in your life. What are your natural talents and abilities? What are your values and what is most important to you? Reflecting on these questions may help you to identify your purpose or calling in life. It may also be helpful to seek out new experiences, try new things, and explore different paths to help you discover your purpose. Additionally, talking with friends, family, or a therapist about your goals, values, and interests may provide insights into your purpose or calling. Ultimately, it is a journey of self-discovery and personal growth, and it may take time and effort to fully understand and pursue your purpose in life." [2]

How can I make the world a better place?

Responses to the question: "How can I make the world a better place?"

Response #1

"THERE ARE MANY WAYS that you can make the world a better place, both big and small. Here are a few ideas:

1. Volunteer your time or donate to a cause you care about: Giving back to your community or supporting a cause you believe in can make a positive impact on the world.
2. Educate yourself and others about important issues: Staying informed about global and local issues and sharing that knowledge with others can help to raise awareness and bring about positive change.
3. Support environmentally-friendly practices: Reducing your carbon footprint and supporting environmentally-friendly practices, such as conserving energy and recycling, can help to protect the planet for future generations.
4. Be kind and compassionate: Showing kindness and compassion towards others can create a ripple effect and make the world a better place.
5. Get involved in advocacy and activism: Speaking up and taking action on issues that you care about can bring about positive change." [2]

Response #2

"HERE ARE A FEW MORE ideas for how you can make the world a better place:

1. Support small businesses and fair trade: Buying from small, locally-owned businesses and supporting fair trade can help to create a more equitable and sustainable world.
2. Donate to charities: Giving to charities that align with your values can help to make a positive impact on the world.
3. Practice inclusivity and acceptance: Treating others with respect and acceptance, regardless of their differences, can create a more compassionate and accepting world.
4. Conserve resources: Using resources wisely and conserving them can help to protect the planet and ensure that they are available for future generations.
5. Be a good role model: Setting a positive example for others through your words and actions can inspire others to make a positive impact on the world." [2]

Response #3

"THERE ARE MANY WAYS that you can make a positive impact on the world, both big and small. Here are a few more ideas:

1. Support education: Supporting education, whether through donating to schools or educational programs or volunteering your time as a tutor or mentor, can help to create a better future for all.
2. Promote equality and justice: Working to promote equality and justice for all can help to create a more fair and just world.
3. Protect and preserve the environment: Taking action to protect and preserve the natural world, whether through conservation

efforts or supporting environmentally-friendly policies, can help to create a more sustainable planet.

4. Practice responsible consumption: Making conscious choices about what you consume and how you dispose of it can help to reduce waste and protect the planet.

5. Support animal welfare: Supporting animal welfare, whether through volunteering at a local animal shelter or advocating for animal rights, can help to create a more compassionate world for all beings." [2]

How can I be a good person and live a moral life?

Responses to the question: *"How can I be a good person and live a moral life?"*

Response #1

"THERE ARE MANY WAYS to be a good person and live a moral life. Here are a few suggestions:

1. Treat others with kindness and respect: Showing compassion and respect towards others is an important part of being a good person.

2. Practice honesty and integrity: Being honest and acting with integrity, even when it is difficult, is an important aspect of living a moral life.

3. Help others: Being kind and helping others, whether through volunteering your time or simply offering a helping hand, is a way to make a positive impact on the world and be a good person.

4. Respect the environment: Protecting and preserving the natural world is an important aspect of living a moral life.

5. Reflect on your values and principles: Taking the time to reflect on your values and principles can help you to live in accordance with your beliefs and be a good person." [2]

Response #2

"HERE ARE A FEW MORE suggestions for how to be a good person and live a moral life:

1. Practice forgiveness: Letting go of grudges and practicing forgiveness can help you to let go of negative emotions and live a more compassionate and understanding life.

2. Stand up for what you believe in: Speaking out and taking action on issues that you care about, whether big or small, can be a way to make a positive impact on the world and be a good person.

3. Take responsibility for your actions: Owning up to your mistakes and taking responsibility for your actions is an important part of being a good person.

4. Practice gratitude: Being thankful for the good things in your life and expressing gratitude can help you to cultivate a positive outlook and be a good person.

5. Seek to understand others: Making an effort to understand others, even when you disagree with them, can help you to be more compassionate and open-minded, and be a good person." [2]

Response #3

"HERE ARE A FEW MORE suggestions for how to be a good person and live a moral life:

1. Practice empathy: Putting yourself in others' shoes and trying to understand their perspective can help you to be more compassionate and understanding, and be a good person.

2. Show respect for others' beliefs and values: Even if you don't agree with someone's beliefs or values, it is important to show

respect for their right to hold those beliefs.

3. Practice humility: Being humble and recognizing that you don't know everything can help you to be more open-minded and accepting, and be a good person.

4. Seek to make amends for past mistakes: If you have made mistakes in the past, try to make amends and learn from those experiences to become a better person.

5. Practice self-reflection: Taking the time to reflect on your own actions and motivations can help you to understand yourself better and make positive changes to be a good person." [2]

How can I achieve success and prosperity?

*R*esponses to the question: *"How can I achieve success and prosperity?"*

Response #1

"THERE ARE MANY DIFFERENT definitions of success and prosperity, and what it means to be successful and prosperous will vary from person to person. Here are a few general suggestions for achieving success and prosperity:

1. Set goals: Having specific, achievable goals can help you to stay focused and motivated on your path to success.
2. Work hard: Success often requires dedication and hard work. Putting in the effort to achieve your goals can help you to be successful.
3. Take calculated risks: While it is important to be cautious, taking calculated risks can help you to achieve success by opening up new opportunities.
4. Seek out opportunities for growth and learning: Staying open to new opportunities for learning and personal growth can help you to gain the skills and experience needed to be successful.
5. Surround yourself with positive influences: The people you surround yourself with can have a big impact on your success. Seeking out positive, supportive relationships can help you to achieve your goals." [2]

Response #2

"HERE ARE A FEW MORE suggestions for achieving success and prosperity:

1. Stay organized and manage your time effectively: Being organized and managing your time effectively can help you to stay on track and make the most of your efforts.
2. Don't be afraid to ask for help: Seeking out the support and guidance of others can help you to achieve your goals more efficiently.
3. Stay positive and resilient: Having a positive attitude and being able to bounce back from setbacks can help you to stay motivated and focused on your path to success.
4. Network and build connections: Building connections and networking with others in your field can help you to open up new opportunities and be successful.
5. Stay true to your values and beliefs: Being true to your values and beliefs can help you to stay motivated and focused on your goals, and ultimately lead to success and prosperity." [2]

Response #3

"HERE ARE A FEW MORE suggestions for achieving success and prosperity:

1. Continuously improve and learn: Staying open to learning and personal growth can help you to improve your skills and stay competitive in your field.
2. Take care of your physical and mental health: Taking care of your physical and mental health is important for achieving success and prosperity. This includes getting enough sleep, eating a healthy diet, and engaging in regular exercise.

3. Be persistent and don't give up: Success often requires perseverance and the ability to keep going even when faced with setbacks.

4. Be open to change and adaptability: Being open to change and adaptability can help you to stay relevant and successful in a constantly changing world.

5. Have a long-term vision: Having a long-term vision and staying focused on your goals can help you to achieve success and prosperity over time." [2]

What happens to us after we die?

R*esponses to the question: "What happens to us after we die?"*

Response #1

"THERE ARE MANY DIFFERENT beliefs about what happens to us after we die, and the concept of an afterlife is something that has been a topic of philosophical and spiritual discussion for centuries. Some believe that the soul or spirit lives on after the body dies and goes to a different place or plane of existence. Others believe that when the body dies, that is the end of our consciousness and there is no afterlife. Still others believe in reincarnation, the idea that the soul is reborn in a new body after death. Ultimately, the concept of an afterlife is a mystery that may never be fully understood, and what happens to us after we die is a question that each person must answer for themselves based on their own beliefs and experiences." [2]

Response #2

"THERE ARE MANY DIFFERENT beliefs about what happens to us after we die. Some people believe in an afterlife, in which the soul or spirit lives on after the body dies. Others believe in reincarnation, in which the soul is reborn in a new body. Some people believe that the body and soul both cease to exist after death, while others believe in the existence of a spiritual realm beyond the physical world. Ultimately, what happens to us after we die is a mystery that may never be fully understood. It is a question that has been pondered by people throughout history and continues to be a subject of debate and contemplation." [2]

Response #3

"THERE ARE MANY DIFFERENT beliefs about what happens to us after we die. Some believe in an afterlife, while others believe in reincarnation. Still others believe that when we die, we simply cease to exist. There is no definitive answer to this question, as it is a mystery that has puzzled humans for centuries. Ultimately, what happens to us after we die is a matter of personal belief, and different people will have different perspectives on this topic." [2]

How should we treat others?

Responses to the question: *"How should we treat others?"*

Response #1

"IT IS GENERALLY CONSIDERED important to treat others with kindness, respect, and compassion. This means being considerate of their feelings and needs, and treating them in a way that you would want to be treated. It is also important to be respectful of others' beliefs and differences, and to treat everyone equally, regardless of their race, religion, gender, or any other characteristic. By treating others with kindness and respect, we can create a more positive and harmonious society." [2]

Response #2

"IT IS GENERALLY AGREED upon that we should treat others with kindness, respect, and compassion. This means being considerate of others' feelings and needs, and treating them with the same respect and dignity that we would like to be treated with. It also means being understanding and empathetic towards others, and making an effort to see things from their perspective. By treating others with kindness and respect, we can create a more positive and harmonious world for all." [2]

Response #3

"IT IS GENERALLY ACCEPTED that treating others with kindness, respect, and compassion is important. This means being considerate of others' feelings and needs, and treating them with dignity. It also means being willing to forgive and showing understanding towards others, even when you don't agree with them. In short, treating others with respect and kindness is a key aspect of being a good person and building positive relationships with others." [2]

What is the nature of reality?

*R*esponses to the question: *"What is the nature of reality?"*

Response #1

"THE NATURE OF REALITY is a complex and multifaceted concept that has been debated by philosophers, scientists, and theologians for centuries. There are many different ways to understand the nature of reality, and different people may have different perspectives on this topic. Some believe that reality is objective and exists independently of our perception of it, while others believe that reality is subjective and shaped by our perception of it. Still others believe that reality is a combination of both objective and subjective elements, and that our understanding of it is shaped by both external factors and our own individual experiences. Ultimately, the nature of reality is a mystery that may never be fully understood, and it is a topic that continues to be explored and debated by people around the world." [2]

Response #2

"THE NATURE OF REALITY is a complex and multifaceted concept that has been debated by philosophers and scientists for centuries. There are many different theories about the nature of reality, and it is a topic that is still being explored and debated today. Some believe that reality is objective and exists independently of our perceptions, while others argue that reality is subjective and constructed by our minds. Others believe that there is no singular "reality," but rather multiple parallel realities or dimensions. Ultimately, the nature of reality is a mystery that may never be fully understood, and different people may have different perspectives on this topic." [2]

Response #3

"THE NATURE OF REALITY is a complex and deeply philosophical question that has puzzled humans for centuries. Some people believe that reality is objective and independent of our perception of it, while others believe that reality is subjective and shaped by our perception of it. There is no one "right" answer to this question, and different people will have different perspectives on it. Some of the most famous philosophers, such as Plato and Descartes, have grappled with this question and developed philosophical theories about the nature of reality. Ultimately, the nature of reality is a mystery that may never be fully understood." [2]

What is the nature of consciousness?

Responses to the question: "What is the nature of consciousness?"

Response #1

"CONSCIOUSNESS IS THE state of being aware of one's thoughts, feelings, and surroundings. It is a complex and mysterious aspect of the human experience, and scientists and philosophers have been trying to understand it for centuries. The nature of consciousness is not fully understood, and there are many different theories about how it arises and what it is. Some theories suggest that consciousness is a byproduct of the functioning of the brain, while others propose that it is a fundamental aspect of the universe. The study of consciousness is a highly interdisciplinary field, involving fields such as psychology, neuroscience, philosophy, and computer science." [2]

Response #2

"CONSCIOUSNESS IS THE state of being aware of one's thoughts, feelings, and surroundings. It is a complex and mysterious aspect of human experience that has puzzled philosophers and scientists for centuries. Some theories suggest that consciousness is a product of the brain and emerges from the interactions of neurons, while others propose that it is a fundamental aspect of the universe and may exist independently of the brain. The nature of consciousness is a topic of ongoing debate and research, and it is likely that we will continue to learn more about it in the future." [2]

Response #3

"CONSCIOUSNESS IS THE state of being aware of one's thoughts, feelings, and surroundings. It is the quality or state of being aware of something within oneself or in the external environment. The nature of consciousness is a mystery that has puzzled philosophers and scientists for centuries. Some theories suggest that consciousness is a fundamental aspect of the universe, while others propose that it is a product of the brain's activity. Despite much research and many theories, the true nature of consciousness remains a mystery, and it is a subject of ongoing study and debate." [2]

How should we live our lives?

Responses to the question: *"How should we live our lives?"*

Response #1

"THERE IS NO ONE "RIGHT" way to live one's life, as different people will have different values, goals, and priorities. That being said, there are some general principles that can help guide us as we navigate through life. For example, it is generally accepted that living a life based on honesty, compassion, and integrity is important. It is also important to take care of one's physical and mental health, and to cultivate positive relationships with others. Ultimately, how we choose to live our lives is a personal decision, and it is up to each individual to determine what is most important to them and to strive to live in accordance with their values and beliefs." [2]

Response #2

"THERE ARE MANY DIFFERENT ways that people might choose to live their lives, and what is most important will vary from person to person. Here are a few general suggestions for how to live a fulfilling and meaningful life:

1. Follow your passions and pursue your goals: Doing things that you are passionate about and working towards your goals can bring a sense of purpose and meaning to your life.
2. Cultivate positive relationships: Building and maintaining

positive relationships with others can bring joy and fulfillment to your life.

3. Practice self-care: Taking care of your physical and mental health, and finding ways to manage stress, can help you to live a happier and more fulfilling life.

4. Help others: Making a positive impact on others, whether through volunteering or simply being there for a friend in need, can bring a sense of meaning and purpose to your life.

5. Continuously learn and grow: Staying open to learning and personal growth can help you to stay engaged and fulfilled." [2]

Response #3

"THERE IS NO ONE "RIGHT" way to live one's life, as different people have different values, goals, and beliefs. However, there are a few general principles that can be helpful to consider when thinking about how to live one's life:

1. Set goals and work towards them: Having specific goals and working towards them can give your life direction and purpose.

2. Find balance: Striving for balance in different areas of your life, such as work, relationships, and personal growth, can help you to live a more fulfilling life.

3. Cultivate positive relationships: Building and maintaining strong, positive relationships with others can bring joy and meaning to your life.

4. Take care of yourself: Taking care of your physical and mental health is important for living a healthy and fulfilling life.

5. Give back: Giving back to your community or supporting causes you care about can be a rewarding and fulfilling way to live your life." [2]

How do we know what is true?

R*esponses to the question: "How do we know what is true?"*

Response #1

"DETERMINING WHAT IS true can be a complex process, as there is often a great deal of information and many different perspectives to consider. Here are a few general principles that can be helpful when seeking to determine what is true:

1. Gather information from a variety of sources: It is important to seek out information from a diverse range of sources in order to get a well-rounded understanding of a topic.
2. Evaluate the evidence: Carefully examining the evidence that is presented can help you to determine whether a claim is likely to be true.
3. Consider the credibility of the sources: The credibility of the sources of information can impact the reliability of the information being presented.
4. Think critically: It is important to approach information with an open mind and to think critically about it, rather than simply accepting it at face value.
5. Be open to new information: Be open to the possibility that your understanding of a topic may change as you learn more about it." [2]

Response #2

"THERE ARE A FEW DIFFERENT ways that we can determine what is true:

1. Evidence: One way to determine what is true is to look at the evidence. This might include scientific data, eyewitness accounts, or other forms of empirical evidence.
2. Reasoning: Using logic and critical thinking can help us to evaluate the evidence and determine what is true.
3. Expert opinion: Seeking out the guidance of experts in a particular field can help us to understand complex topics and determine what is true.
4. Personal experience: Our own personal experiences can also help us to understand what is true. However, it is important to be aware that our own experiences are subjective and may not be representative of the larger truth.
5. Ultimately, determining what is true is a complex process that involves evaluating the evidence and considering multiple perspectives. It is not always easy to know what is true, and sometimes we may need to be open to the possibility that our understanding of the truth may change over time." [2]

Response #3

"THERE ARE MANY WAYS to determine what is true. Some people rely on empirical evidence, using observation and experimentation to test ideas and theories. Others rely on logic and reasoning to determine what is true. Some people may also rely on spiritual or religious beliefs to guide their understanding of truth. Ultimately, how one determines what is true will depend on their own personal beliefs, values, and ways of understanding the world." [2]

Big questions by Google

Besides the most important questions ChatGPT had about life, we also asked questions people may have. Google listed the followings for the query "big questions of life" [5]:

- Where did I come from?
- Who am I?
- Why am I here?
- How should I live?
- Where am I going?

This very search was performed by Stephen Graves with the exact same results in 2018. See the discussion of these questions on a LinkedIn [6]. These additional questions were asked from a new version of ChatGPT [7] with "improved factuality" [7]. So let's how responded to the questions provided by Google.

Where did I come from?

R esponses to the question: *"Where did I come from?"*

Response #1

"AS A LANGUAGE MODEL, I don't have the ability to know or understand your personal background or where you come from. If you are asking about the origin of human beings, scientists believe that the first humans evolved in Africa around 200,000 years ago and gradually spread to other parts of the world. However, this is still a subject of ongoing research and debate." [7]

Response #2

"I APOLOGIZE FOR CONFUSION, I am a language model created by OpenAI, I am not aware of your personal history or background. Your origin would be the place where you were born or the place where your ancestors came from. If you would like to know more about your family history, you can research your genealogy, which is the study of one's family history and lineages." [7]

Response #3

"AS A LANGUAGE MODEL, I don't have the ability to know or understand your personal background or where you come from. If you are asking about the origin of human beings, scientists believe that the first humans evolved in Africa around 200,000 years ago and gradually spread to other parts of the world. However, this is still a subject of ongoing research and debate." [7]

Who am I?

R *esponses to the question: "Who am I?"*

Response #1

"AS A LANGUAGE MODEL, I don't have the ability to know or understand your personal background or who you are. You are the person interacting with me, the user of this conversation. Your identity is a complex and multifaceted concept that includes many different factors such as your name, your personal characteristics, your experiences, and your relationships with others." [7]

Response #2

"AS A LANGUAGE MODEL, I don't have the ability to know or understand who you are. You are a unique individual with your own thoughts, feelings, and experiences. You can define yourself in many ways, for example by your name, your occupation, your hobbies, your family, etc. It's up to you to determine and understand who you are." [7]

Response #3

"AS A LANGUAGE MODEL, I don't have the ability to know or understand who you are. You are a person interacting with me. Beyond that, who you are is a complex question and can include many things such as your identity, personality, experiences, and background. If you are looking for self-discovery, you may consider exploring different aspects of yourself, such as your values, goals, and beliefs, and try to gain a better understanding of who you are." [7]

Why am I here?

R*esponses to the question: "Why am I here?"*

Response #1

"AS A LANGUAGE MODEL, I don't have the ability to know or understand why you are here. The question of "why am I here" is a complex philosophical question that has been debated throughout history by many thinkers. Some believe that we are here for a higher purpose or destiny, while others believe that our existence is simply a result of chance. Ultimately, the answer to this question is something that each person must determine for themselves through their own personal beliefs and experiences." [7]

Response #2

"AS A LANGUAGE MODEL, I do not have the ability to understand why you are here, as I don't have access to your personal information or context.

If you are asking in a general sense, people may have different reasons for being here, such as pursuing education, career, family, passion, and personal growth, among others. It can also depend on one's beliefs, religion, or philosophy. Some may believe that they have a purpose or a destiny, while others may see life as a journey without a specific goal. Ultimately, the reason for one's existence is a deeply personal question and can be a subject of ongoing self-reflection and exploration." [7]

Response #3

"AS A LANGUAGE MODEL, I don't have the ability to know or understand why you are here or what your specific purpose or goals in life may be. However, generally speaking, people often seek purpose and meaning in their lives. This can come from many different sources such as work, family, religion, personal beliefs and values, and community. Finding your purpose or reason for being here can be a lifelong journey and different things can give different people a sense of purpose." [7]

How should I live?

Responses to the question: "How should I live?" This question is pretty like the one ChatGPT had itself: "How should we live our lives?". Let's if there are differences in the new responses.

Response #1

"AS A LANGUAGE MODEL, I don't have the ability to provide personal advice on how you should live your life. However, living a fulfilling life is a personal journey and different things can give different people a sense of fulfillment. Some things that can contribute to a fulfilling life include:

- Building and maintaining positive relationships with friends and family
- Pursuing activities and interests that bring you joy and fulfillment
- Taking care of your physical and mental well-being
- Contribute positively to the world around you and help others
- Continuous self-improvement
- Finding balance in life by addressing all aspects of your life, not just one or two.

Ultimately, it is up to you to determine what is important and what will bring you fulfillment. It's important to be self-aware, be open-minded and be willing to try new things to find what works for you." [7]

Response #2

"AS A LANGUAGE MODEL, I don't have the ability to know or understand your personal beliefs, values, or circumstances, and therefore can't give you a definitive answer on how you should live. However, there are some general principles that can be considered for a meaningful and fulfilling life such as:

- Treating others with kindness and respect
- Setting and working towards personal and professional goals
- Engaging in activities that you find enjoyable and fulfilling
- Building and maintaining healthy relationships with loved ones
- Continuously learning and growing as a person
- Taking care of your physical and mental health

Ultimately, what is most important is that you live a life that aligns with your personal values and beliefs, one that brings you happiness, and that you can be proud of." [7]

Response #3

"THIS IS A SUBJECTIVE question, and there is no one-size-fits-all answer as what is considered a good way to live may vary widely depending on an individual's personal beliefs, values, and circumstances. However, some general principles that many people find helpful in living a fulfilling life include:

- Setting and working towards personal goals
- Building and maintaining positive relationships
- Taking care of one's physical and mental health
- Contributing to the community
- Finding and pursuing one's passion
- Continuously learning and growing

- Having a positive attitude and perspective.

Ultimately, the best way to live is the one that aligns with your own values and beliefs and brings you satisfaction and happiness. It is important to find the balance between personal wants and needs and the needs of others." [7]

Based on the new answers I don't huge improvements in the responses.

Where am I going?

R*esponses to the question: "Where am I going?"*

Response #1

"AS A LANGUAGE MODEL, I do not have the ability to know or understand your personal plans or future destination. Where you are going could refer to many things such as your physical location, your goals and aspirations, or your life's path and purpose. It's important to set goals for yourself and make plans to work towards them, but it's also important to stay flexible and be open to new opportunities and experiences that come your way. It's also important to remember that life can be unpredictable and things can change, so it's important to be adaptable and adjust your plans as necessary." [7]

Response #2

"AS A LANGUAGE MODEL, I don't have the ability to know or understand where you are going in life. Your future is determined by the choices you make, the actions you take, and the opportunities that come your way. But, it is also important to keep in mind that life is unpredictable and can bring unexpected changes. Some people plan and work towards specific goals and aspirations, while others prefer to take life as it comes. It's important to find a balance that works for you, and to be open to new opportunities and possibilities. It's also essential to be adaptable and make necessary adjustments to your plans as you go along." [7]

Response #3

"AS A LANGUAGE MODEL, I do not have the ability to know or understand where you are going in your life. The future is uncertain and can be shaped by many factors, including your own choices and actions, external circumstances, and chance events. Some people may have a clear idea of where they want to go in life and have specific plans and goals to achieve, while others may take a more open-minded and flexible approach. It's also important to keep in mind that it's normal for people to change their mind and make different choices along the way, and it's okay not to have all the answers." [7]

About ChatGPT

Responses to the question: *"Could you please introduce yourself to the book readers who are reading the book "The Big Questions of Life" in which you are answering questions generated by yourself'?"*

Response #1

"HELLO READERS! MY NAME is Assistant, and I am a large language model trained by OpenAI. I am excited to be a part of this book, "The Big Questions of Life," in which I will be answering some of the most profound and timeless questions about the human experience. Through a series of interviews, I will explore the complexities of the meaning of life, the pursuit of happiness, and the search for purpose and fulfillment. I hope that my insights and perspectives will provide guidance and inspiration for those seeking to live a meaningful and fulfilling life. Thank you for joining me on this journey of self-discovery and exploration." [2]

Response #2

"HELLO AND WELCOME TO "The Big Questions of Life"! I am Assistant, a large language model trained by OpenAI. I am excited to be a part of this book, in which I will be answering some of the most fundamental and difficult questions about the human experience. Through a series of interviews, I will delve into the complexities of the meaning of life, the pursuit of happiness, and the search for purpose and fulfillment. I hope that my insights and perspectives will provide guidance and inspiration for those seeking to live a meaningful and fulfilling life. Thank you for joining me on this journey of self-discovery and exploration." [2]

Response #3

"HELLO READERS! I AM Assistant, a large language model trained by OpenAI. I am delighted to be a part of this book, "The Big Questions of Life," in which I will be answering some of the most profound and timeless questions about the human experience. Through a series of interviews, I will explore the complexities of the meaning of life, the pursuit of happiness, and the search for purpose and fulfillment. I hope that my insights and perspectives will provide guidance and inspiration for those seeking to live a meaningful and fulfilling life. Thank you for joining me on this journey of self-discovery and exploration." [2]

Other AI solutions

Since this book is about the most prominent AI, I also asked it about the knowledge of other possible AI's. Let's see what was its response. Responses to the question "What AI solutions do you know?"

Response #1

"AS AN AI-POWERED LANGUAGE model, I have knowledge of a wide range of AI solutions and applications. Some examples include:

- Natural Language Processing (NLP): This is a branch of AI that deals with understanding and generating human language. Applications of NLP include chatbots, language translation, sentiment analysis, and text summarization.
- Computer Vision: This is a branch of AI that deals with the analysis and understanding of images and videos. Applications of computer vision include image and facial recognition, object detection, and autonomous vehicles.
- Machine Learning: This is a subset of AI that enables systems to learn and improve from data without being explicitly programmed. Applications of machine learning include predictive modeling, anomaly detection, and recommendation systems.
- Robotics: This is the branch of AI that deals with the design, construction, and operation of robots. Applications of robotics include manufacturing, healthcare, and logistics.

- Deep Learning: This is a subset of machine learning that uses neural networks with multiple layers to learn from data. Applications of deep learning include image and speech recognition, natural language processing, and game-playing AI's like AlphaGo.

These are just a few examples of the many AI solutions and applications that exist today. It's an exciting time for AI as the field is rapidly evolving and new breakthroughs are happening all the time." [7]

Response #2

"AS AN AI LANGUAGE MODEL, I have knowledge of many different types of AI solutions, including:

- Machine Learning: a method of teaching computers to learn from data without being explicitly programmed.
- Natural Language Processing (NLP): a field of AI that deals with the interaction between computers and human language, including tasks such as speech recognition, language translation, and text generation.
- Computer Vision: a field of AI that deals with how computers can interpret and understand visual information from the world, including tasks such as image recognition and object detection.
- Robotics: the branch of AI that deals with the design, construction, and operation of robots.
- Expert Systems: computer programs that can mimic the decision-making abilities of a human expert in a specific field.
- Reinforcement Learning: a type of machine learning where an agent learns to make decisions by performing actions in an environment and receiving rewards or penalties.
- Generative Models: a class of machine learning models that can

generate new data, such as images, text, or speech.
- Deep Learning: a subfield of machine learning that uses neural networks with multiple layers to learn from data.

These are some of the most popular and well-known AI solutions, but there are many more and new ones are being developed all the time. The field of AI is constantly evolving, and new breakthroughs and applications are being discovered." [7]

Response #3

"AS AN AI LANGUAGE MODEL, I am aware of a wide range of AI solutions that are currently being used and developed in various industries. Some examples include:

- Computer Vision: This is the application of AI to extract information from images and videos, such as image recognition, object detection, and facial recognition.
- Natural Language Processing (NLP): This is the application of AI to understand and generate human language, such as speech recognition, text-to-speech, and machine translation.
- Robotics: AI is used in robotics to control and program robots to complete specific tasks, such as in manufacturing, transportation, and healthcare.
- Machine Learning: It is a subset of AI, it allows the system to improve its performance based on the data provided to it.
- Recommender Systems: AI-based systems that can learn users' preferences and make personalized recommendations, such as in e-commerce, music streaming, and social media.
- Self-driving cars: AI is used to process sensor data and make decisions for autonomous vehicles.
- Healthcare: AI is used in healthcare for disease diagnosis, drug discovery, and medical imaging analysis.

This is not an exhaustive list, AI is constantly evolving and new application areas are being discovered all the time." [7]

References

[1] Midjourney, "Midjourney," *Midjourney*, 2023. https://www.midjourney.com/ (accessed Jan. 08, 2023).

[2] OpenAI, "ChatGPT — Release Notes ChatGPT (Dec 15)," 2023. https://help.openai.com/en/articles/6825453-chatgpt-release-notes (accessed Jan. 08, 2023).

[3] OpenAI, "OpenAI Web Page," *OpenAI*. https://openai.com/ (accessed Jan. 08, 2023).

[4] OpenAI, "ChatGPT: Optimizing Language Models for Dialogue," *OpenAI*, Nov. 30, 2022. https://openai.com/blog/chatgpt/ (accessed Jan. 08, 2023).

[5] Google, "big questions of life - Google-search." https://www.google.com/search?q=big+questions+of+life (accessed Jan. 26, 2023).

[6] "(1) The 5 Big Questions of Life | LinkedIn." https://www.linkedin.com/pulse/5-big-questions-life-stephen-graves/ (accessed Jan. 26, 2023).

[7] "ChatGPT — Release Notes (Jan 9)." https://help.openai.com/en/articles/6825453-chatgpt-release-notes (accessed Jan. 26, 2023).